TABLE OF CONTENTS

SECRETS OF SUCCESSFUL STUDENTS

The Secret Power of Psychology

Successful Students know thoughts are things.

If thoughts are things, it makes sense to make sense of things.

The fastest way Successful Students make sense of their thought-things is by acknowledging how they think of something determines how the thing behaves, whether that thing is a person, place or thing.

Successful Students obviously make the most of their thoughts, and choose to focus on how things have a relationship to them, in one way or another.

Perspective comes in handy when Successful Students want to know what nouns are true and which are false.

There are 7 billion multiple choice answers in life.

Successful Students know this, and therefore maintain a healthy, detached perspective when they are staring at a blank word document.

Instead of being fooled by the illusion of separation when observing some thing with their mind's eye, Successful Students know every effect has a cause, is connected, and is worth a closer look.

Successful Students love to learn.

Successful Students take responsibility for the things in their lives that both make sense, and the things that do not readily.

This is how Successful Students navigate their boats to relative calm in the rough storms of the seven seas known as school.

What Can Psychology Do For You?

_____

_____

_____

_____

_____

_____

_____

_____

_____

_____

_____

_____

_____

_____

_____

_____

How Your Mind Makes You Happy

Successful Students make themselves happy.

They do not wait around looking for their friends and classmates to make them happy.

Successful Students enjoy staying late in the art studio.

Without happiness and contentment, nothing means anything anyway; not good grades, honors, scholarships, first prize.

Successful Students are thankful when they pass a test, or receive some tutoring from a peer or a professor.

Successful Students always see the silver lining surrounding the dark clouds of despair and desperation.

There are always midterms to study for, there are always opportunities to get a groove on, always new people to meet, and the sun always rises.

Successful Students use their minds to make themselves happy by knowing how nothing can last.

They look at bad marks as an opportunity to improve, instead of a chance to give up and throw in the towel.

Successful Students make their own luck by being prepared, so when the opportunity arises, they snatch it up and make it seem easy.

School is a neutral place, like most places in life.

Successful Students' secret to happiness on the last day of midterms? They take everything one step at a time.

How Can Your Mind Help You To Be Happy?

How Your Mind Makes You Healthy

Successful Students know they are what they eat.

Food is fuel, and just as their thoughts determine their success at school, their thoughts influence what they eat, when they eat, and how they eat.

Physical Successful Students are motivated towards achievement, and see doors where others see only walls.

The more Successful Students achieve, the more they believe they will achieve, and no surprise, the more they achieve.

When nature balances itself out with some spring clearning, Successful Students are not caught off guard. If they go on a bender, they come out the other side a little older and wiser.

The mind of a Successful Student is one of balance, moderation and sobriety.

Healthy thoughts lead to healthy choices.

Healthy thoughts lead to good grades and good jobs.

Healthy thoughts lead to lasting relationships.

This is why Successful Students are successful.

Successful Students believe in stimulating and challenging their minds, a gift not to be taken for granted.

Successful Students learn new languages, play musical instruments, travel during their time off, because new experiences excite them and stimulate their taste buds, motivating them to eat and think their way to a long life.

How Can Your Mind Help You To Be Healthy?

_____

_____

_____

_____

_____

_____

_____

_____

_____

_____

_____

_____

_____

_____

How Your Mind Makes You Wealthy

Successful Students become wealthy because they balance their wants and needs with the balance in their chequing accounts.

Successful Students also save what money they can because they know about compound interest and the benefit of starting their higher education or retirement fund early.

The more Successful Students learn, the more they earn.

Successful Students have part-time jobs to supplement their student loans, savings or tuition fund.

Books and pub crawls eat up extra cash fast, so Successful Students supplement their income with work-study positions that keep them involved in their area of expertise, as well as earn them a bit of money.

Successful Students are in the minority of lifelong learners; they are the self-made millionaires of the world.

As soon as they are experts, they go and learn something new.

Successful Students keep their minds and their options open.

Ready to pounce, Successful Students are alert to opportunities for entrepreneurship on and around campus, for their fellow students have unmet needs Successful Students can fulfill.

Successful Students are regularly tutors, newspaper publishers, entertainers or vendors of goodies edible and otherwise.

Money comes easily to Successful Students because when they give back to society and their communities, their cups overflow with not just money, but other forms of wealth too.

How Can Your Mind Help You To Be Wealthy?

How Your Mind Makes You Popular

Successful Students are in the right place at the right time.

High achievers seek extra credit, and make lemonade when faculty gives them lemons.

Successful Students step out of their comfort zones and take social risks, instead watching and waiting for someone else to make them rich, famous, popular, intelligent and wordly.

If they see an opportunity to point a lost student in the right direction, they gladly jump at the chance.

If they see an opportunity to volunteer for a social or political event on campus that excites them or they are curious about, they dive right in.

Successful Students know how there is safety in numbers and work towards bringing people together for common causes and projects.

If it appears Successful Students have few friends, they are surely being stimulated off-campus. They are on campus for one reason and one reason only: to get their degree.

Successful Students naturally make friends easily, because they see no need to be anything but themselves.

Successful Students support Successful Students in achieving their goals, and this is why they are one big happy family, their relationships strengthening over time, often into old age.

Belief in their ability to connect and communicate with other people is how Successful Students make friends. They trust themselves and they trust others.

How Can Your Mind Help You To Be Popular?

_____

_____

_____

_____

_____

_____

_____

_____

_____

_____

_____

_____

_____

_____

_____

How Your Mind Makes You Smart

Successful Students want to succeed on their midterms, so when it comes time to study, they study.

Study now, party later is the opposite of buy now, pay later.

Successful Students put time, money and energy into their education, because this improves everything in their lives.

Good grades help Successful Students get where they want to go, faster than if they just floated along without direction and without a purpose.

Because Successful Students are happy, healthy and have friends, their genetic make-up is somehow altered in a way that predisposes them to get better grades.

And good grades lead to good grades.

Successful Students are always improving their study skills, because achieving comes naturally to them.

They desire to prove to themselves they are worthy of the accolades that accompany student success.

Successful Students revel in positive attention and celebrate being celebrated by their peers, professors, colleagues, faculty, friends and family.

Successful Students practice the tasks and skills, activities, experiments and sports they want to be good at.

And the more they practice, the smarter Successful Students get at the subjects that interest them, the sports they rock and the creative projects they love to create.

How Can Your Mind Help You To Be Smart?

How Your Mind Makes You Sexy

Successful Students have charisma.

Charisma is an energetic inner glow that originates from enthusiasm, joy, and passion for learning.

Successful Students get dates.

They get dates because active, keen and alert minds are in demand, like all desirable traits.

Successful Students are sexy.

And it is no surprise that Successful Students attract Successful Students.

Successful Students feed off of the success of people like them.

The mind of a Successful Student is a steel trap; they remember names, dates, faces and due dates.

Everyone likes it when someone remembers their name, especially when that person is an attractive member of the opposite sex.

Dating leads to marriage and partnerships, which only enhance the power, potential and productivity of Successful Students.

Still, there are only so many times Successful Students can read the same book or edit a term paper, so it behooves them to take breaks and loosen up.

Successful Students know that Shakespeare is not going anywhere, so when that special someone sends them a text message, they follow the beckon of the birds and the bees.

14

How Can Your Mind Help You To Be Sexy?

_____

_____

_____

_____

_____

_____

_____

_____

_____

_____

_____

_____

_____

_____

_____

_____

_____

How Your Mind Makes You Free

Successful Students are party animals, just not every night.

Successful Students build international empires to serve, support and celebrate the wants, needs, wishes and dreams of other people, then they party to celebrate the achievement of their grand goals.

Successful Students are the ones who sail around the world because they believe they can.

The more alive and willing to express themselves they are, the more capable they are of getting down and letting loose.

Boogie-woogie is the name of the game for high achievers.

Because they know how to have fun, every other project in the back of their lockers and their minds gets done, and on time.

Successful Students balance homework and playtime easily.

And their friends support them, because they are Successful Students too; birds of a feather flock together.

The life of the party, Successful Students are rarely falling down drunk, but when they do, their friends look after them and make sure they get back home safe.

As long as Successful Students believe they are capable of juggling freedom and finals, they are role models for their peers. Commitment and responsibility allow for freedom.

Because Successful Students know they are free to do what they do with ease, and are the few who do, they are often the envy of the many, who are waiting for who knows what.

How Can Your Mind Help You To Be Free?

_____

_____

_____

_____

_____

_____

_____

_____

_____

_____

_____

_____

_____

_____

The Secret Power of Physiology

Successful Students know they manifest their thoughts through their bodies.

Everything begins in the body.

It is with their bodies that Successful Students are able to be successful, and get through school in the first place.

Successful Students know the power of their physiology and work out, exercise, eat fruit and vegetables and take care of themselves.

Bodies are vehicles and Successful Students keep their vehicles in top running condition.

Regular service and maintenance is crucial to optimum performance, so regular check-ups and healthy choices, not only at the grocery store, but also at the pub are signs of Successful Students.

Physiology is the study of body functions. Every part of a Successful Student's body is a machine and needs the proper fuel, in the right amount, at the right time.

Good thing Successful Students are aware of their body and its role in their personal and professional development, both in the classroom and on the track.

Successful Students look after their bodies because they care about how they feel, how they look, how they function and desire a long and happy life in a vehicle that will get them from A to B, and beyond.

Strong, healthy Successful Students accomplish amazing feats.

What Can Physiology Do For You?

_____

_____

_____

_____

_____

_____

_____

_____

_____

_____

_____

_____

_____

_____

How Your Body Makes You Happy

Successful Students are products of their environment.

They are affected by, and affect what goes on around them.

Exercise gets Successful Students naturally high; this is how they get their ya-yas out.

Successful Students know there is no better way to keep their bodies in top physical shape than to regularly run, walk, swim, row, jump, wrestle, ride, lift, throw, kick, push and pull.

Even when injuries threaten to slow Successful Students down, their conditioned and toned bodies have adapted to change, allowing faster recovery times.

Successful Students feel good and therefore perform well.

Successful Students have zest and energy, so they are happy.

Successful Students are a pleasure to be around, because they exude confidence and poise. Nothing is beyond the reach of movers and shakers like these.

Always willing to give advice and support to those who wish to improve their lives, other people flock to Successful Students because their physical ability and attention to their health makes them irresistible.

Without a happy body, there is no way Successful Students could be happy.

Successful Students spend their time, money and energy improving their physiology, and the rewards are well worth the effort; the proof is in the pudding.

How Can Your Body Help You To Be Happy?

_____

_____

_____

_____

_____

_____

_____

_____

_____

_____

_____

_____

_____

How Your Body Makes You Healthy

Successful Students know the only way they can lead countries, businesses, meetings and workshops is with their bodies.

The more Successful Students look after their bodies, the more their bodies look after them.

Successful Students stay to the outside aisles at the grocery store, because all the packaged products in the middle are trying to kill them.

Successful Students drink plenty of water everyday, and eat organic fruits and vegetables, because they are healthier.

A healthy body can work wonders. Successful Students are the engines of progress in the fields of technology, art, food, medicine, business and entertainment.

Regardless of the genes Successful Students are born with, they overcome difficulties by the healthy choices they make.

Bodies are machines that love to have their engines revved.

Successful Students fill themselves with energy in the forms they most prefer and because they care about their bodies.

Successful Students know how their bodies can heal themselves.

Bodies replace and regrow and regenerate by the second.

Such finely-tuned powerhouses of energy, Successful Students give their bodies what they need to succeed and are given the gift of longevity and immunity in return.

How Can Your Body Help You To Be Healthy?

_____

_____

_____

_____

_____

_____

_____

_____

_____

_____

_____

_____

_____

_____

How Your Body Makes You Wealthy

Successful Students can attain wealth, turn the tide, and make a dime with their charm, chutzpa, charisma and old-fashioned focused action.

Their bodies are specifically designed for hard work, and the Successful Students who make the most of this physical blessing are those who are blessed with the fattest bank accounts.

Money comes to Successful Students when they work towards serving their communities in some way.

Filling a need or helping someone get where they want to go always brings rewards to Successful Students willing to go the extra mile, take some initiative and take the bull by the horns.

Bodies are created to be actively seeking fulfillment.

Action gets Successful Students where they want to go.

Nothing can be substituted for action.

Without action, nothing of value can be created or maintained.

And if nothing of value is created or maintained, wealth in all its forms is just is not there.

Successful Students believe in creating value in society, because creating value goes with the territory of being a Successful Student.

Everything a Successful Student does in some way creates value for at least their circle of influence, if not ripples that influence the whole world.

How Can Your Body Help You To Be Wealthy?

_____

_____

_____

_____

_____

_____

_____

_____

_____

_____

_____

_____

_____

How Your Body Makes You Popular

Successful Students make friends with their bodies first.

Then they make friends with other Successful Students who have made friends with their own bodies.

Happy, healthy, friendly bodies everywhere are hard to resist, looking from across the lecture hall.

Leadership is needed and Successful Students heed the call.

With toned muscles, shiny hair and smooth skin, it is easy to see why effort in the physical fitness department pays off.

Successful Students are willing to invest in their body.

This is what sets Successful Students apart from others.

A key ingredient in the success of any Successful Student's relationship is the ability to honor and respect their temple.

Shaping up is in every Successful Student's benefit, because leaving anything to chance allows for entropy to take over and once that happens, it becomes harder to regain the vitality and vigor of youth.

Friends are worth more than gold to Successful Students, and their bodies help them get through the stress of school life.

By celebrating their bodies, Successful Students put themselves in an enviable position. Successful Students are popular.

Not only do their bodies outlast others, they are also able to keep up with other Successful Students in pursuing their dreams to the ends of the earth, and soon, far into outer space.

How Can Your Body Help You To Be Popular?

How Your Body Makes You Smart

The reason Successful Students are smart is because they keep their bodies in good shape.

Successful Students are able to study longer, harder, faster, easier and study better. Endurance and smarts support each other when it comes to achieving the impossible.

This is no mistake; without keeping everything in balance, Successful Students would not be Successful Students.

By adeptly adapting to their environments, their bodies overcome the pressure of deadlines and competition.

The more their grades motivate Successful Students, the more they are driven to improve their physical health.

If only for the reason of being more productive at their school work and their part-time jobs, Successful Students know what they want and go and get it.

To Successful Students, their bodies are sacred sites.

They take and teach yoga classes, run marathons, participate in tests of endurance, race other Successful Students and go for the gold in everything they do.

They are able to achieve whatever they set their minds to.

Good grades are just the beginning.

Proof of the unlimited ability of super-achievement, Successful Students are the wonders of the world, making it all look easy; behind the scenes they are putting in the effort required, because nothing worthwhile is easy.

How Can Your Body Help You To Be Smart?

_____

_____

_____

_____

_____

_____

_____

_____

_____

_____

_____

_____

_____

_____

_____

_____

How Your Body Makes You Sexy

Successful Students take the long way around; short cuts do not exist to these people.

The more Successful Students work on maintaining their physical health and appearance, the more attractive they are to the opposite sex.

And attractiveness to the opposite sex is handy when it comes to getting dates, and Successful Students have no trouble when it comes to interesting a suitor.

Successful Students are flooded with emails, invitations and text messages, all from admirers, near and far.

The Successful Students who keep their bodies in shape get asked out on the most dates.

No surprise, a great body is an asset worth a million bucks.

Successful Students instinctively know this; they know how to take care of themselves, inside and out.

They know what makes them feel good and what makes them feel bad, and are the strongest and fittest people on earth.

Successful Students get this way by knowing what they want.

Achievement is sexy, as is power, confidence and ability.

While people are sitting on the couch watching television wondering why telemarketers are the only people who call, Successful Students are either at the gym, in the library, on the track, at a party surrounded with adoring fans, or managing all their friends on facebook, of which there are many; sex sells.

How Can Your Body Help You To Be Sexy?

_____

_____

_____

_____

_____

_____

_____

_____

_____

_____

_____

_____

_____

_____

How Your Body Makes You Free

Successful Students know their bodies are especially resilient, especially while they are young.

Successful Students can party, eat and drink, smoke and rock and roll all night, but in the morning, back to school they go.

Successful Students are quite aware of the effects of too much of anything, including entertaining a false sense of freedom, and have the wisdom beyond their years to steer clear of any excess that will knock them and their dreams off balance.

Bodies can only take so much abuse, and an ounce of prevention is worth a pound of cure, so Successful Students take this advice to heart, and take it easy when substance use flirts with abuse.

Successful Students would rather die than harm their bodies.

Successful Students need a body to party, and because they look ahead and plan for the long-term, they ultimately choose to abstain from too much hoopla, because tomorrow always comes, and they never feel that great with a hangover.

Everything in moderation.

Physiological well-being is at the root of every great accomplishment, and Successful Students have no need to go overboard, because they are so thrilled and enchanted by their ability to let their hair down on an occasional basis.

There is no need to become addicted to the illusion of freedom.

Successful Students have bigger plans, and are implementing them while other people are waking up still drunk.

How Can Your Body Help You To Be Free?

_____

_____

_____

_____

_____

_____

_____

_____

_____

_____

_____

_____

_____

_____

_____

The Secret Power of Spirituality

Successful Students are connected to their sense of spirit, however they choose to interpret and name it.

Spirituality is the glue that holds the Secret of Successful Students together.

Without a spiritual base from which to operate, there is little meaning to being a Successful Student in the first place.

Psychology and Physiology are both incredibly important aspects of Successful Students, though without the guiding force of Spirituality behind them, they might as well be going in circles.

Successful Students use spirituality to navigate when they cannot readily see an outcome to their thoughts and actions.

A sense of spirituality helps Successful Students see in the dark, and have faith their needs will be met as they journey on the path to self-realization and self-actualization.

Successful Students know they are here to serve the greater good with their gifts, knowledge, wisdom, projects, creativity, brains, brawn and good looks.

The power of spirituality is crucial to all success, helping Successful Students become whole.

Spirituality is the light at the end of tunnel, allowing them to trust in the unknown when they are faced with uncertainty.

Successful Students solve the mysteries of their lives by having faith in a higher power; these people also benefit by allowing other people to believe what they want to believe.

What Can Spirituality Do For You?

_____

_____

_____

_____

_____

_____

_____

_____

_____

_____

_____

_____

_____

_____

How Your Spirit Makes You Happy

Successful Students celebrate their spirituality every chance they get, because it brings them a sense of joy and purpose.

Spirit makes Successful Students happy, because by celebrating the work of spirit in their lives, they are able to succeed in any subject they choose.

Honors make Successful Students happy.

Spirit knows all the answers.

Successful Students know this, and have no trouble allowing their spirit to lead the way.

Spirit enriches the lives and loves of Successful Students.

Their connection to spirit is their secret to success at school.

It does not get simpler than this.

Spirit helps Successful Students feel worthy and deserving and on purpose and on time, no matter what challenges they face.

When Successful Students get good grades or win a scholarship, they know they succeeded because the power of spirit was behind them all the way.

Spirit infused their minds and bodies with the confidence and persistence they needed, when they needed it.

Successful Students are always willing to serve their higher purpose, because they know there is meaning to their lives and they are eager to do their best; even if it is not always clear as to what their higher purpose is, they trust in their spirit.

How Can Your Spirit Help You To Be Happy?

_____

_____

_____

_____

_____

_____

_____

_____

_____

_____

_____

_____

_____

How Your Spirit Makes You Healthy

Successful Students are inspired, in spirit.

They look after their bodies, because their bodies are the vehicle for their spirit to manifest its glory in the world.

Successful Students take care of themselves, because a fine physical form is an unstoppable force here on earth.

A happy spirit is a healthy spirit.

Successful Students know they came from a spiritual place.

Successful Students know they belong in a healthy body.

Successful Students know the only way to channel the light, love, healing, power and fun available to all, is to tone their vehicle, keep the tires filled with air, gas in their tank, their headlights on, and a map on their laps.

The invisible energy of spirit is healing and nurturing.

Successful Students know there is no need to push or pull or get or grab or struggle for what they desire.

Successful Students allow their spirit to work through them in whatever ways their spirit chooses.

Successful Students do not ask questions of spirit, knowing all is in divine order.

Perfect health comes when Successful Students get acquainted with their spirit in a deep and personal way; this is how they find their way when the power goes out in the library or the cafeteria.

How Can Your Spirit Help You To Be Healthy?

_____

_____

_____

_____

_____

_____

_____

_____

_____

_____

_____

_____

_____

_____

_____

_____

How Your Spirit Makes You Wealthy

Successful Students become wealthy by appreciating wealth.

Wealth is a bi-product of being on purpose and providing value, in whatever way feels natural.

Successful Students give value to their communities by following their spirit's guidance; volunteer efforts of time, energy and money improve both their own situation, and the situations of others.

Spirit always provides Successful Students with the resources they need to do the work of spirit.

Wealth means much more than money.

Successful Students have a wealth of peace and contentment.

Successful Students have a wealth of healthy relationships.

Successful Students can be wealthy with an abundance of brains, sex appeal, or the gift of musical or sports talent.

How wealth is measured by others does not even register on the radar of Successful Students.

Successful Students are more concerned with how they can serve their families, their friends, their communities, their countries, their continents, and the world at large.

Focusing on spiritual wealth is how Successful Students are able to accomplish their straight A's, among other success.

Focusing on spiritual wealth is how Successful Students are able to do anything they set their minds, bodies and hearts to.

How Can Your Spirit Help You To Be Wealthy?

_____

_____

_____

_____

_____

_____

_____

_____

_____

_____

_____

_____

_____

_____

How Your Spirit Makes You Popular

In the grand scheme of things Successful Students win the popularity contest hands down; results speak volumes.

If for some reason they have not found instant and immediate popularity at school, chances are they are destined for immense popularity once they have matured like a vintage fine wine.

Successful Students will have plenty of opportunities to enjoy the riches and rewards of popularity once they have completed their school work, obtained a degree or three, and are in the enviable position to really blossom into movers and shakers.

Some Successful Students are late bloomers, thankfully.

Successful Students do not burn bright, wither and die.

Successful Students are guided by spirit, follow the inner guidance they receive, and intend on showing the world just how powerful aligning with spirit can be.

Infused with almost infinite power it seems, it takes little for a Successful Student to be popular.

Success is will always be popular.

Success is sexy.

Even so, at the end of the day, vain popularity is hollow and shallow, and leaves even Successful Students with the notion there is something greater out there.

There is.

And it lasts longer than time or money or parties or popularity.

How Can Your Spirit Help You To Be Popular?

How Your Spirit Makes You Smart

Successful Students believe in the timeless knowledge of their spirit, which is naturally all-knowing.

Successful Students are not afraid to ask their spirit for guidance, no matter what the obstacle is in their way.

Smart students are Successful Students and Successful Students are smart students.

Spirit and smarts go hand in hand. They are not alone, separate, disconnected or afraid of each other.

In fact, both rely upon the other, and exist because of each other.

Spirit creates everything out of nothing, and created every Successful Student out of the same stuff everything else was created out of.

Pretty smart.

Successful Students have tapped into this knowing too, and connect with spirit whenever their exams all seem to be blurring into each other, or their coach is pushing them to do better, run or row or swim faster, jump higher or throw farther.

Successful Students infuse every bit of their school work and extra-curricular activities with spirit.

This just makes sense to them, not needing to analyze or quantify or decide either way.

Successful Students are smart because their spirit made it so, and there is no reason to doubt infinite intelligence.

How Can Your Spirit Help You To Be Smart?

How Your Spirit Makes You Sexy

Knowing they have a spirit makes a Successful Student sexy.

Sex appeal comes from an inner glow and an outer electricity that shows up whenever Successful Students are on purpose.

And Successful Students could not be on purpose without knowing and honoring their special connection to their spirit.

Sex appeal is a product of harmonizing body, mind and spirit.

Successful Students are sexy because they see the relationship of these three pillars of life in everything they do.

Body, mind and spirit are inter-related and inter-connected.

Successful Students live in the present.

Successful Students juggle their thoughts and actions with their inner guidance, just like mind, body and spirit need to work together in harmony for maximum benefit and effect.

Nothing happens alone; spirit, mind and body are all sexy.

Knowing spirit so intimately, Successful Students do what needs to be done in the classroom, in the studio and on the playing field.

They are co-creators who channel their passion and enlightened ideas into inspired action and amazing solutions.

Creativity and productivity are the sexiest characteristics on the planet, and their spirit holds the key to this secret.

Successful Students know all the secrets.

How Can Your Spirit Help You To Be Sexy?

_____

_____

_____

_____

_____

_____

_____

_____

_____

_____

_____

_____

_____

_____

_____

_____

How Your Spirit Makes You Free

Successful Students are free from fear because they have faith.

They have faith in the power and potential of their spirit that sustains their faith in the face of any challenge.

Guidance from the divine creative source itself allows Successful Students to follow their dreams without fear of failure.

Because failure does not exist.

Successful Students know this, and this is why they are not scared to try new things, move across the country to go to school, or enroll in a class they know nothing about.

But every action they take leads to knowing either something works or it does not; this social freedom is invaluable.

Knowing this, Successful Students have a better understanding of what it takes to get where they want to go.

Not dissuaded or bummed out because something turned out another way, they learn from false starts and mis-takes.

Successful Students feel free to try new things.

Believing they are capable of achieving their goals and realizing their dreams, Successful Students know they have the power of their spirit guiding them in all they undertake.

With spirit as their co-pilot, nothing is impossible.

Maybe it ultimately takes them a little more time or effort, but what else is life for?

How Can Your Spirit Help You To Be Free?

_____

_____

_____

_____

_____

_____

_____

_____

_____

_____

_____

_____

_____

_____

Published by: SnowbirdBooks.com

ISBN: 978-0-9948468-5-3

If you found this book and spent the time to read it,
and answer the questions, you have what it takes
to become (or continue being) a Successful Student.

I believe in you. But so do you :)

That is why you picked it up in the first place.

Good luck!

Oliver

Email me: OliverLukeDelorie@Gmail.com